Editor
Erica N. Russikoff, M.A.

Editor in Chief
Ina Massler Levin, M.A.

Creative Director
Karen J. Goldfluss, M.S. Ed.

Illustrator
Mark Mason

Cover Artist
Barb Lorseyedi

Art Coordinator
Renée Mc Elwee

Imaging
Leonard P. Swierski

Publisher
Mary D. Smith, M.S. Ed.

GRADES 3-4

TCR 2980

READING COMPREHENSION *ACTIVITIES*

PREDICTING
SEQUENCING
COMPARING & CONTRASTING
INFERENCING
VISUALIZING
MAKING CONNECTIONS
DISCOVERING THE MAIN IDEA
SUMMARIZING
RECOGNIZING CAUSE & EFFECT
DESCRIBING THE SETTING ...AND MORE

Covers key skills and strategies

Provides suggested reading lists for each section

Contains creative critical-thinking activities for individuals, small groups, or the whole class

Includes standards and benchmarks

Teacher Created Resources

D1568593

Authors
Jennifer Cripe, M.S. Ed.
Angela Vetter, M.S. Ed.

Teacher Created Resources
6421 Industry Way
Westminster, CA 92683
www.teachercreated.com
ISBN: 978-1-4206-2980-4
© 2011 Teacher Created Resources
Made in U.S.A.

Teacher Created Resources

Table of Contents

Introduction

Reading is an essential component throughout education. It enables students to be successful in all areas of the curricula. Comprehension is a skill that is necessary to create a love of reading, something that all teachers want for students. This book, *Reading Comprehension Activities*, provides teachers with engaging activities to teach the fundamental strategies and skills that build reading comprehension. This book focuses on the following specific reading strategies and skills:

Strategies	Skills	
• Predicting	• Summarizing	• Setting
• Context Clues	• Sequencing	• Problem and Solution
• Inferencing	• Retelling	• Compare and Contrast
• Visualizing	• Main Idea	• Cause and Effect
• Making Connections	• Characterization	

Reading Comprehension Activities contains a variety of activities for each of the different strategies and skills listed. Activities include teacher modeling, small group and center interactive work, and independent practice. These activities will enhance students' learning and can be used as a supplement to any core reading program. Many of the activities within this book allow teachers to use personal literature choices, giving the opportunity to provide differentiated instruction. A suggested book list is given at the beginning of each strategy or skill section. These books support the activities in each section.

Reading Comprehension Activities is designed to provide meaningful practice with the essential skills needed to succeed in reading. While students are actively engaged in these literacy activities, they will be challenged and will develop skills to apply to any independent reading selection.

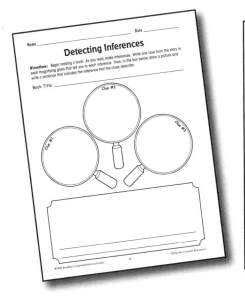
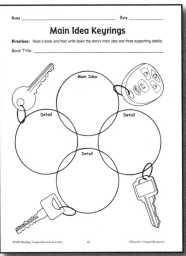
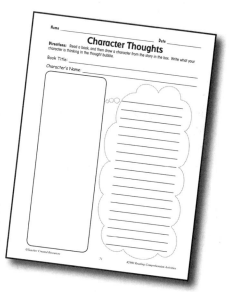

Standards and Benchmarks

Each activity in *Reading Comprehension Activities* meets at least one of the following standards and benchmarks, which are used with permission from McREL. Copyright 2011 McREL. Mid-continent Research for Education and Learning. 4601 DTC Boulevard, Suite 500, Denver, CO 80237. Telephone: 303-337-0990. Website: *www.mcrel.org/standards-benchmarks.* To align McREL Standards to the Common Core Standards, go to *www.mcrel.org.*

Standards and Benchmarks	Activity	Page(s)
Standard 5. Uses the general skills and strategies of the reading process		
Benchmark 1. Previews text (e.g., skims material; uses pictures, textual clues, and text format)	Book Cover Predictions	8
	Making Predictions	9
	Stop, Think, Predict	10
Benchmark 3. Makes, confirms, and revises simple predictions about what will be found in a text (e.g., uses prior knowledge and ideas presented in text, illustrations, titles, topic sentences, key words, and foreshadowing clues)	Book Cover Predictions	8
	Making Predictions	9
	Stop, Think, Predict	10
Benchmark 5. Uses a variety of context clues to decode unknown words (e.g., draws on earlier reading, reads ahead)	Finding the Clues	13–15
	Context Clue Cards	16–17
	Buggin' Out with Context Clues	18–19
Benchmark 6. Uses word reference materials (e.g., glossary, dictionary, thesaurus) to determine the meaning, pronunciation, and derivations of unknown words	Finding the Clues in Sentences	15
Standard 6. Uses skills and strategies to read a variety of literary texts		
Benchmark 1. Reads a variety of literary passages and texts (e.g., fairy tales, folktales, fiction, nonfiction, myths, poems, fables, fantasies, historical fiction, biographies, autobiographies, chapter books)	All activities	All activity pages
Benchmark 3. Understands the basic concept of plot (e.g., main problem, conflict, resolution, cause and effect)	Monkeying Around with a Problem	79
	Problem and Solution Cookie Jars	80–81
	Problems and Solutions in the Sky	82
Benchmark 4. Understands similarities and differences within and among literary works from various genres and cultures (e.g., in terms of settings, character types, events, point of view; role of natural phenomena)	"Y" Not Compare?	85
	Creamy Comparisons	86
	Sea Animal Comparisons	87–88
	Cause and Effect Map	91
	What Caused It?	92
	Cause and Effect Matchup Cards	93–95

Standards and Benchmarks *(cont.)*

Standards and Benchmarks	Activity	Page(s)
Standard 6. *(cont.)*		
Benchmark 5. Understands elements of character development in literary works (e.g., differences between main and minor characters; character's point of view; stereotypical characters as opposed to fully developed characters; changes that characters undergo; the importance of a character's actions, motives, and appearance to plot and theme)	Character Faces Visualizing a Character Character Thoughts	69 70 71
Benchmark 8. Makes connections between characters or simple events in a literary work and people or events in his or her own life	This Reminds Me . . . Connecting to Characters Connection Cards	35 36 37–38
Standard 7. Uses skills and strategies to read a variety of informational texts		
Benchmark 5. Summarizes and paraphrases information in texts (e.g., includes the main idea and significant supporting details of a reading selection)	"HIP" Summaries Summary Signs "What Happened?" Chapter Summaries Main Idea Keyrings "Egg"cellent Main Ideas Main Ideas from Outer Space	41–42 43 44 62 63–64 65–66
Benchmark 6. Uses prior knowledge and experience to understand and respond to new information	All activities	All activity pages
Benchmark 7. Understands structural patterns or organization in informational texts (e.g., chronological, logical, or sequential order; compare and contrast; cause and effect; proposition and support)	Sarah Gets Ready for School Sequence-a-Story Booklet Squiggly Sequencing Sweet Retellings Fly Away with Retellings Retelling, from Seed to Sprout "Y" Not Compare? Creamy Comparisons Sea Animal Comparisons Cause and Effect Map What Caused It? Cause and Effect Matchup Cards	47–48 49–51 52 55–56 57–58 59 85 86 87–88 91 92 93–95

©*Teacher Created Resources*   5   *#2980 Reading Comprehension Activities*

Predicting

This strategy is crucial, as it makes students become more aware and attentive readers. In this section, teachers can help their students find clues in the text to make and revise predictions. Whether looking at the cover of a book or finding proof in the text, students will become masters at making genuine predictions. The following reproducible pages can be used with any book, so students can practice predicting in different ways!

Suggested Books for Teaching Predicting

dePaola, Tomie. *Strega Nona's Magic Lessons.* New York: Harcourt, 1982.
Anthony gets into trouble after trying to use Strega Nona's magic.

Long, Melinda. *How I Became a Pirate.* San Diego, CA: Harcourt, 2003.
Jeremy thinks that being a pirate is fun; however, he eventually misses the comforts of home.

Munsch, Robert. *Paper Bag Princess.* Toronto: Annick Press, 1980.
Elizabeth is a beautiful princess who is about to live "happily ever after" with Prince Ronald until a dragon gets in the way.

Munson, Derek. *Enemy Pie.* San Francisco, CA: Chronicle Books, 2000.
Jeremy moves into a new neighborhood and becomes "Enemy #1." Fortunately, Dad knows how to help—with pie!

Swope, Sam. *Araboolies of Liberty Street.* New York: Farrar, Straus and Giroux, 1989.
General Pinch is in charge of his gray, fun-free neighborhood—that is, until the highly spirited Araboolies arrive.

Activities for Predicting

Book Cover Predictions

Copy Book Cover Predictions (page 8) for each student. Choose any picture book that provides enough detail on the cover so that students can give clear predictions. Share the cover of the book. Have students examine the cover and write their predictions in the box. Then ask students to support their predictions by writing down the hints the cover gave them that led them to the predictions they made.

Making Predictions

This activity allows students the opportunity to revisit their predictions. To begin this activity, choose any picture book or text the students are assigned to read. Then copy Making Predictions (page 9) for each student. Preview the text with students and provide them with a chance to write predictions, as well as time to explain their reasons for the predictions. After reading the selected pages, students can then check their predictions and use examples from the text to confirm their guesses. With practice, students will become great prediction makers!

Stop, Think, Predict

This activity will help students learn to use clues from the text of any book in order to make predictions. Begin by copying Stop, Think, Predict (page 10) for each student. Using a selected passage, students will preview the text for clues that will guide them in making predictions. Have students write down their predictions and, after reading the text, check their guesses to see whether they were correct and why. Your students will not be able to "stop" predicting after this activity!

Name _____ Date _____

Book Cover Predictions

Directions: Look at the cover of a book. In the box, predict what the story will be about. Write the reasons for your prediction on the lines below the box.

Book Title: _____

By looking at the cover of this book, I think the story is going to be about . . .

_____

_____

_____

_____

_____

_____

_____

_____

_____

_____

Hint 1 _____

_____

Hint 2 _____

_____

Hint 3 _____

_____

Name _____ Date _____

Making Predictions

Directions: Briefly preview a book. Write the book title, two predictions, and your reasons for these predictions on the lines below. Then tell whether you were correct or incorrect, and why.

Book Title: _____

My first prediction: _____

_____

I think this because _____

_____

My first prediction was _____ (correct, incorrect) because the book told me:

_____

_____

_____

_____

My second prediction: _____

_____

I think this because _____

_____

My second prediction was _____ (correct, incorrect) because the book told me:

_____

_____

_____

_____

Name _____   Date _____

Stop, Think, Predict

Directions: Briefly preview a book. Before you write down your predictions of what you think will happen, write down the clues that led you to your predictions. Then tell whether you were correct or not, and why.

Book Title: _____

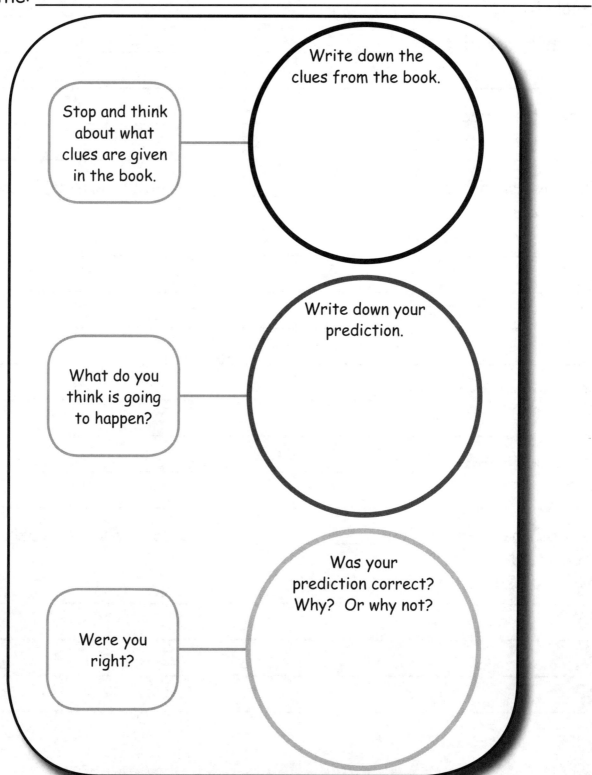

Context Clues

In this section, teachers will find creative context clue activities for students to practice this necessary strategy. By being alert to context clues, students can find the meanings of unfamiliar words, increasing their vocabulary and overall reading comprehension. With the following activities, teachers can model the correct way to use surrounding words in order to understand tricky text.

Suggested Books for Teaching Context Clues

Barrett, Judi. *Pickles to Pittsburgh.* New York: Atheneum, 1997.
Kate and Henry anxiously await Grandpa's return from his vacation. In the meantime, Grandpa's postcard has Kate's imagination running wild.

Gibbons, Faye. *Night in the Barn.* New York: HarperCollins, 1995.
A young boy, his big brother, and their two cousins spend the night in a barn. Not even their flashlight can keep away the shadowy monsters they see.

Palatini, Margie. *Broom Mates.* New York: Hyperion, 2003.
Gritch the Witch is preparing for her Halloween party. Will her sister, Mag the Hag, be a help or a hindrance?

Scieszka, Jon. *Baloney (Henry P.).* New York: Puffin, 2005.
Henry is late to *szkola,* or school, once again. Before blasting off to class, he comes up with one crafty story to tell his teacher, Miss Bugscuffle.

Yolen, Jane. *Piggins.* New York: Harcourt, 1987.
Piggins, a butler, ends up being the star of an elite dinner party when he solves a crime that took place that evening.

Activities for Context Clues

Finding the Clues . . .

In this activity, you will first model how to find clues in a reading passage using Finding the Clues in Passages (page 13). First, copy the teacher model so that each student has a page to look at. Read the teacher sample aloud and review with students the clues that the text gives for the meanings of the underlined words. Then pass out copies of the student version of Finding the Clues in Passages (page 14) and a highlighter (or crayons) to each student. The students will highlight (or underline) the clues that helped them figure out the meaning of the underlined words. For extra practice, copy and hand out Finding the Clues in Sentences (page 15) to students. This sheet invites students to predict the meaning of words using context clues. After writing down their guesses, students will see if they are correct by looking up the corresponding dictionary definitions.

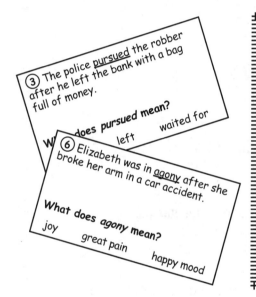

③ The police pursued the robber after he left the bank with a bag full of money.

What does pursued mean?

left   waited for

⑥ Elizabeth was in agony after she broke her arm in a car accident.

What does agony mean?

joy   great pain   happy mood

Context Clue Cards

These context clue cards are an engaging way for students to practice this essential reading strategy. To begin, copy Context Clue Cards (page 16) onto cardstock and laminate for durability. Cut out the cards. Then copy Context Clue Cards Recording Sheet (page 17). Give each student one recording sheet. Students will use context clues to find the meaning of the underlined word in each sentence. Once they figure out which one fits, they will write it on the recording sheet.

Buggin' Out with Context Clues

Copy Buggin' Out with Context Clues, preferably using red construction paper for page 19 and white paper for page 18. Students will use context clues to match the words on the ladybug to the meanings on the black spots. Have students cut out the spots. Students will glue the black spots to the ladybug—but only at the top of the spots so that they can be lifted for assessment. For fun, students can cut out the ladybugs and display them on a bulletin board titled "Buggin' Out with Context Clues."

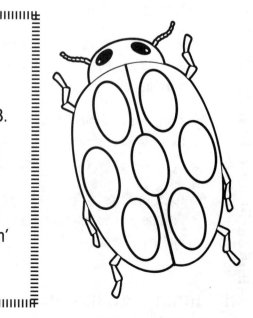

Finding the Clues in Passages

Teacher Model

Directions: Read each passage below. Look at the underlined word in each passage. Highlight the words in each passage that give clues to finding the meaning of the underlined word. Then write the meaning of the underlined word on the lines.

Mark and Henry couldn't wait for the night to come. They had been studying the moon and the stars in their second grade class. Finally, when night came, the stars and the moon were clearly visible. The sky was clear of night clouds, so the stars shone brightly like lights in a stadium. The moon was beaming amidst the darkness of the sky. Henry and Mark were excited to see the moon and stars so easily.

Paula and her little son, Matt, went to the store to buy a gift. As they were shopping, Matt left his mother's side to hide in the clothing rack. When Paula looked down, she saw that Matt was missing. She became frantic as she searched for her missing son. She raced up and down the aisles of the store until Matt popped out from under a rack and yelled, "Here I am!"

Visible means _____

_____

Frantic means _____

_____

Finding the Clues in Passages *(cont.)*

Directions: Read each passage below. Look at the underlined word in each passage. Highlight the words in each passage that give clues to finding the meaning of the underlined word. Then write the meaning of the underlined word on the lines.

1. Jason is trying to <u>locate</u> the library book that he lost last week. Jason and his brother have looked in their rooms and in their backpacks. They have both checked the toy room and their desks at school. Jason is very worried that he will never find the book.

Locate means _____

2. During our class field trip, a boy named Bobby forgot his lunch on the bus. As we all found a seat for lunch at the park, our teacher was trying to <u>resolve</u> Bobby's problem. She figured out a way for Bobby to eat because other students wanted to share their lunches.

Resolve means _____

3. Sarah went shopping with her friend, Emily. As they went from store to store, buying new outfits, Emily saw a pretty white <u>tunic</u>. She thought about how well the tunic would go with her new denim skirt. The new outfit would be great to wear for the first day of school.

Tunic means _____

4. The pirates on the ship have <u>sought</u> a huge treasure chest that is full of gold and jewels. For months, they have been searching for this treasure on many islands. Finding this treasure would mean great riches for all the pirates aboard the ship!

Sought means _____

Finding the Clues in Sentences

Directions: Read each sentence and write down what you think the underlined word means. Then add what clues were in the sentence that helped you decide this. Use a dictionary to look up each word's meaning. Then compare your answers with the dictionary definitions.

1. The rotten eggs left in the kitchen had a <u>pungent</u> smell that filled the room.

What I think it means: _____

Clues from the sentence: _____

Dictionary definition: _____

_____

2. Sammy was upset because his teacher <u>detained</u> him after school, and he was late for baseball practice.

What I think it means: _____

Clues from the sentence: _____

Dictionary definition: _____

_____

3. Lisa walked into her brother's <u>filthy</u> room, which was covered in dirty laundry and garbage.

What I think it means: _____

Clues from the sentence: _____

Dictionary definition: _____

_____

4. Brady helped his dad <u>navigate</u> their way through the woods using his Boy Scout compass and trail map.

What I think it means: _____

Clues from the sentence: _____

Dictionary definition: _____

_____

Context Clue Cards

① The sun was hiding behind the dark gray clouds that covered the sky. It seemed <u>dreary</u> outside without the sunlight.

What does *dreary* mean?

    warm   wild   sad

② As we sat in our chairs outside, we <u>gazed</u> up at the stars and moon.

What does *gazed* mean?

    jumped   looked   sang

③ The police <u>pursued</u> the robber after he left the bank with a bag full of money.

What does *pursued* mean?

    chased   left   waited for

④ Jimmy is always very <u>wary</u> of strange animals. He is worried that he might get bitten.

What does *wary* mean?

    careful   playful   happy

⑤ I forgot my lunchbox at home and, when it was lunchtime at school, I was <u>famished</u>. I could hear my stomach growl.

What does *famished* mean?

    hungry   sick   rich

⑥ Elizabeth was in <u>agony</u> after she broke her arm in a car accident.

What does *agony* mean?

    joy   great pain   happy mood

⑦ I waited patiently for my birthday party to begin. I was <u>eager</u> to play with my friends and open my presents!

What does *eager* mean?

    sad   grumpy   very excited

⑧ We have to be quiet in the library as we read books. Talking loudly can <u>disturb</u> other people who are reading.

What does *disturb* mean?

    clean   bother   help

⑨ Henry tried to <u>salvage</u> all the pieces he could find of his project after it fell off the table and broke. He wanted to put it back together.

What does *salvage* mean?

    save   give away   destroy

⑩ Jill had a bruise on her knee after falling off her bike. She tried to <u>conceal</u> the bruise by wearing pants.

What does *conceal* mean?

    show   hurt   hide

Context Clue Cards
Recording Sheet

Directions: Read each numbered card. Use context clues to figure out the meaning of the underlined word. Write the meaning of the underlined word next to the number that matches the number on the card.

1. _____ 6. _____

2. _____ 7. _____

3. _____ 8. _____

4. _____ 9. _____

5. _____ 10. _____

✂ ▬

Name _____ Date _____

Context Clue Cards
Recording Sheet

Directions: Read each numbered card. Use context clues to figure out the meaning of the underlined word. Write the meaning of the underlined word next to the number that matches the number on the card.

1. _____ 6. _____

2. _____ 7. _____

3. _____ 8. _____

4. _____ 9. _____

5. _____ 10. _____

Buggin' Out with Context Clues

Directions: Look at each "spot" carefully. The words shown are the definitions for the underlined words on the ladybug. (See page 19.) Find the meanings of the underlined words using context clues. Match the spots to the sentences on the ladybug. Cut out the spots and glue the tops of them to the correct sentences on the ladybug.

huge

noise

went down

chew

pain

moved quickly

jumped

Buggin' Out with Context Clues *(cont.)*

The bugs began to <u>gnaw</u> at the bark that was lying in the yard.

Yikes! That bug just <u>hurdled</u> over my bed.

The <u>enormous</u> bug scared me.

The bees flew over our heads and created a <u>vibration</u>.

After a few days, the bug bite <u>descended</u> and disappeared.

The bright yellow bug <u>scampered</u> across the floor.

The bug bite created <u>discomfort</u> in my arm. Ouch!

Inferencing

Making inferences can be a very difficult but rewarding strategy for children to master. This section provides activities that will help students form conclusions based on textual clues. Students will use interactive matching or analyzing activities that can be done in a small group or a whole-class setting.

Suggested Books for Teaching Inferencing

Aardema, Verna. *Why Mosquitoes Buzz in People's Ears: A West African Tale.* New York: Dial Press, 1975.
Do you ever wonder why mosquitoes make that buzzing sound? It's explained in this animal-and-insect African tale.

Golenbock, Peter. *Teammates.* San Diego, CA: Harcourt, 1990.
Legendary baseball player Jackie Robinson had to face many things in his lifetime, but when he joined the Dodgers, he was faced with something very different: brotherhood.

Ringgold, Faith. *Tar Beach.* New York: Crown Publishers, 1991.
"Tar Beach" is the paved Harlem apartment rooftop where Cassie's family goes to picnic and dream of what they hope to have in the future.

Soto, Gary. *Too Many Tamales.* New York: Putnam, 1993.
Maria is helping her mother make tamales for the holidays. When her mother's ring goes missing, there's only one thing Maria can do—eat!

Van Allsburg, Chris. *Two Bad Ants.* Boston: Houghton Mifflin, 1988.
While in search of sugar for their queen, two ants find themselves on their own kitchen adventure.

Activities for Inferencing

Author Hints

Copy Author Hints (page 22) for each student. Select a book that allows students to make good inferences and provides author "hints." As students read, they will make inferences and write them in the "My Inferences" column. Then students will write down phrases or sentences that describe their inferences in the "What the Author Tells Me" column.

Guess the Setting Cards

This engaging matching activity will help students become experts at making inferences about the setting. To begin, copy Guess the Setting Cards (pages 23–24) onto cardstock and laminate for durability. Cut out the cards and place them into an envelope. Then copy Guess the Setting Cards Recording Sheet (page 25), one per student. Students will need to match the rectangular description cards to the appropriate circular setting cards. After matching the cards, students will record their answers next to the corresponding numbers on the recording sheet. They will also summarize the hints from the description that helped them decide on the place. Then students will create their own "Where Am I?" riddles, which can be shared with other students and can provide a good discussion about inferences.

Detecting Inferences

This activity will help your little detectives find clues in texts in order to make good inferences. Copy Detecting Inferences (page 26) for each student. Choose any book that allows students to make good inferences. As you read aloud, students will discuss the inferences that they made. In the magnifying glasses, they will need to write the clues that the author provided that support their inferences. At the bottom of the page, students will draw pictures of what the clues describe and write detailed sentences that explain their clues.

Author Hints

Directions: Begin reading a book. Write down your inferences from the book in the "My Inferences" column. Write down phrases or sentences that led you to your inferences in the "What the Author Tells Me" column.

Book Title: _____

My Inferences	What the Author Tells Me

Guess the Setting Cards

① We enter a dark hole. It's cold and musty, and it feels very damp inside. We listen closely and can hear the sound of bats hanging above.

Where are we?

② There is light everywhere. The smell of cotton candy is making me hungry. The Ferris wheel is full of happy people.

Where am I?

③ The waves crash against the coast. The smell of salt water fills my nose. The seagulls soar above me.

Where am I?

④ The slides are huge, and the swings look like fun. I can hear kids yelling and screaming with joy.

Where am I?

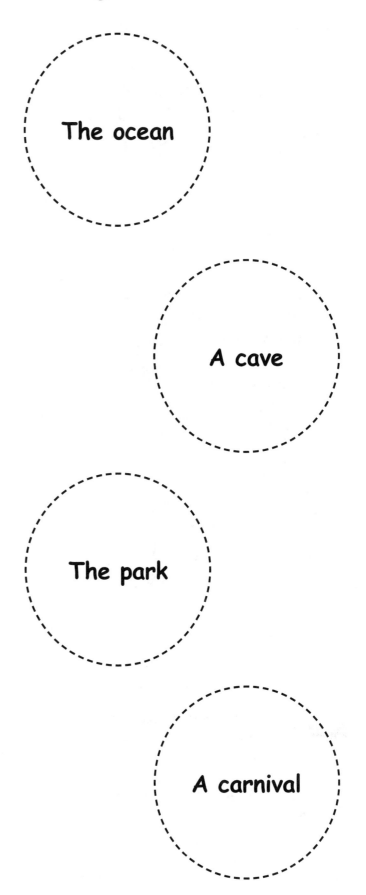

The ocean

A cave

The park

A carnival

Guess the Setting Cards *(cont.)*

⑤ The tumbleweeds blow in front of us as we walk on the dry, cracking dirt. We feel hot and thirsty.

Where are we?

A restaurant

⑥ Kids are wearing cone-shaped hats and playing many games. We sing songs, and one kid blows out candles. It's so much fun!

Where are we?

The desert

⑦ The door slams behind me. My mom tells me to put on my seat belt. The engine begins to rev. We're off!

Where are we?

A birthday party

⑧ The waiter comes to our table and asks me if I would like something to drink. I answer, "Milk, please!"

Where am I?

A car

Name _____   Date _____

Guess the Setting Cards
Recording Sheet

Directions: Read the cards. Match the description of the place (the rectangular cards) to the place you think it best describes (the circular cards). When you have matched all eight cards, write each place next to the number that matches the number on the rectangular card. Then briefly summarize the hints that helped you decide on the place.

Place Where You Are	Hints Given
1. _____	_____
2. _____	_____
3. _____	_____
4. _____	_____
5. _____	_____
6. _____	_____
7. _____	_____
8. _____	_____

Directions: Create your own "Where Am I?" riddle. Describe a setting in the box below. Then write your place in the circle. Cut out both shapes and add them to those of other students for a new game.

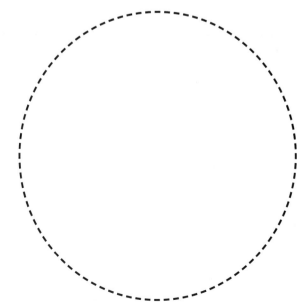

Name _____   Date _____

Detecting Inferences

Directions: Begin reading a book. As you read, make inferences. Write one clue from the story in each magnifying glass that led you to each inference. Then, in the box below, draw a picture and write a sentence that includes the inference that the clues describe.

Book Title: _____

Clue #2

Clue #1

Clue #3

_____
_____

Visualizing

Visualizing can make reading come alive for young readers. In this strategy section, students will be able to use their imaginations to help create "mind pictures" of what happens in the stories they read. Teachers can instruct students how to use their senses to fully experience the text, as well as to use graphic organizers with any chosen text.

Suggested Books for Teaching Visualizing

Day, Alexandra. *Good Dog, Carl.* New York: Simon & Schuster, 1985.
   Carl, an adorable Rottweiler, dutifully watches over a baby while Mom is gone.

Fleischman, Paul. *Weslandia.* Cambridge, MA: Candlewick Press, 1999.
   Wesley is spending his summer doing something other children won't be doing—he is caring for a unique and wondrous plant.

Gibbons, Faye. *Night in the Barn.* New York: HarperCollins, 1995.
   A young boy, his big brother, and their two cousins spend the night in a barn. Not even their flashlight can keep away the shadowy monsters they see.

Swope, Sam. *Araboolies of Liberty Street.* New York: Farrar, Straus and Giroux, 1989.
   General Pinch is in charge of his gray, fun-free neighborhood—that is, until the highly spirited Araboolies arrive.

Yolen, Jane. *Owl Moon.* New York: Philomel Books, 1987.
   On a moonlit winter night, a girl and her father take a walk and look for owls.

Activities for Visualizing

What's the Cover?

To help students begin to imagine what a book might be about, copy What's the Cover? (page 29) for each student. Select a picture book with a great title that will allow students to visualize scenes from the book. Read the title of the book aloud to the students, while not showing them the cover. Then have students draw a detailed picture describing the title of the book and what they think may happen.

Making Mind Pictures

This activity will help students learn how to think about different events and imagine what is happening in texts. Copy Making Mind Pictures (page 30) for each student. Choose a picture book to read aloud or use a guided reading text for this activity. Have students write about a certain part of the book and then draw a picture of what they visualized as they read. In a small group, students can share their pictures and describe what they saw. This is a concrete and effective way to show students how to use the visualization strategy during their own reading!

What Do You See?

This fun activity will help your students envision different scenes. Copy "What Do You See?" Cards (page 31) onto cardstock and laminate for durability. Cut out the cards. Then copy What Do You See? (page 32) for each student. For this activity, students will select one of the scene cards and read it carefully. As they read, students will imagine what is happening and draw detailed pictures of what is going on in the text. Afterwards, they will write sentences describing their pictures. This activity will really get imaginations working!

What's the Cover?

Directions: Listen to your teacher as he or she tells you the title of a book. Draw a new cover for the book with a detailed picture that describes its title.

Book Title: _____

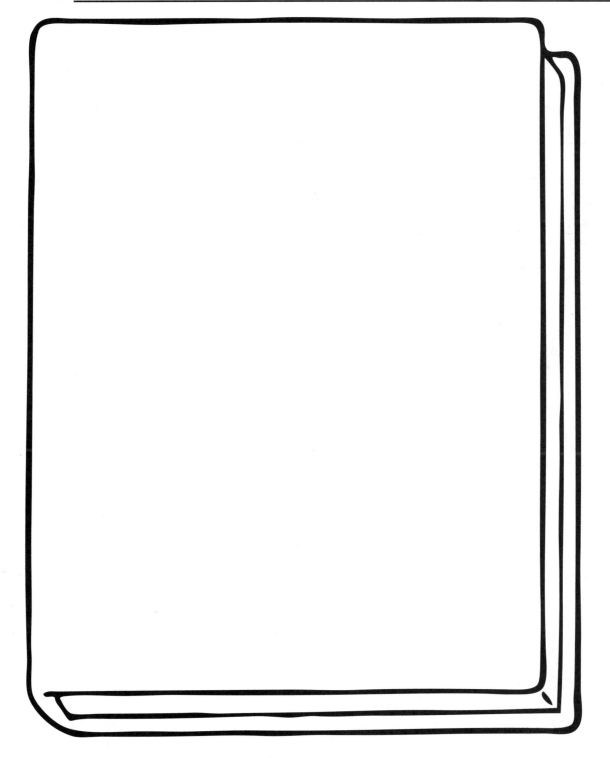

Name _____   Date _____

Making Mind Pictures

Directions: After you've started reading a book, write a short description of what you have read. Use this description to help you draw a detailed picture of the reading.

Book Title: _____

Author: _____

I read about: _____

_____

_____

_____

I pictured . . .

"What Do You See?" Cards

Card #1

The party was so much fun! James had many friends at his ninth birthday party. He couldn't believe it! His mom decorated the house with bright balloons and colorful streamers. The presents were piled high on the table next to the cake covered in a sugary frosting. All his friends were busy playing games or finishing their pizza. Soon, it would be time to try to break open the piñata. James was very excited!

Card #2

The beach was a beautiful place. The sky was free of clouds, and the sun shone brightly. The soft, crumbly sand felt great beneath my feet. Along the shore, some kids were building a sand castle, a few grown-ups were reading books, and a man was throwing a Frisbee® to a dog. I found a place to set down my beach towel and chair. I looked out at the ocean and watched some people surfing as I sipped my lemonade. What a day to relax!

Card #3

As Sarah walked through the woods, she noticed a small deer taking a drink from a creek. Sarah hid behind one of the tall pine trees and watched the deer quietly. Behind the creek and among many trees was a tiny cabin with smoke coming from the chimney. Sarah guessed that someone was home. Just then, a thin man with a gray beard walked out the front door, grabbed a stack of firewood, and went back inside. After the deer galloped away, Sarah moved closer to the creek and sat on a large rock to rest for a while.

Card #4

As Kyle walked onto his new school playground, he felt afraid. Kyle was shy and did not know how to make friends. He could hear all the kids laughing and giggling. He saw groups of kids playing kickball on the field and others playing on the slides. Some girls were jumping rope. Kyle walked slowly toward the four-square game, which he loved. He watched others for a moment. Just then, a nice boy asked, "Would you like to play?"

Name _____ Date _____

What Do You See?

Directions: Read one of the "What Do You See?" cards to yourself and try to imagine what is happening in the story. Write down the card number, and draw a picture of what you see in your mind. Afterwards, write a sentence describing your picture.

Card # _____

_____

_____

_____

_____

Making Connections

This strategy is essential to the success of any reader. With different types of graphic organizers, teachers can effectively help their students relate to texts on many levels. Students can practice making connections with connecting-to-text question cards and will learn to relate to texts through text-to-text, text-to-self, and text-to-world connection activities.

Suggested Books for Teaching Making Connections

Cowan, Catherine. *My Life with the Wave.* New York: HarperCollins, 1997.
    A boy brings home a wave as a pet, only to discover it is unruly and must be returned to the sea.

dePaola, Tomie. *Oliver Button Is a Sissy.* New York: Harcourt, 1979.
    When Oliver decides to be in the talent show, his classmates call him a "sissy." He may not win a trophy at the show, but he wins something more valuable: acceptance.

Fox, Mem. *Wilfrid Gordon McDonald Partridge.* Brooklyn, NY: Kane/Miller Book Publishers, 1985.
    Wilfrid is a young boy who befriends 96-year-old Miss Nancy. Upon discovering that she has lost her memory, he helps her find it.

Polacco, Patricia. *Chicken Sunday.* New York: PaperStar Books, 1992.
    A girl and her two best friends make decorative eggs in order to raise enough money to buy the boys' grandma her favorite hat.

Rylant, Cynthia. *The Relatives Came.* New York: Atheneum, 1985.
    The anticipation is growing as the relatives are coming to visit for a welcome family reunion.

Activities for Making Connections

This Reminds Me . . .

This graphic organizer can be used with any text. Begin by copying This Reminds Me . . . (page 35) for each student. Students can read any selected story or book, and as they read, they can make personal responses to the text. Have your students write about the part in the text that helped them make a connection. Also, have them describe what kind of connection it is. This is a great way for them to practice making connections!

Connecting to Characters

With this activity, your students will be able to practice making connections with characters from their stories. Select a text to read that is filled with varied character personalities. Then make one copy of Connecting to Characters (page 36) for each student. After reading the chosen text, have students complete the questions on the page and draw a picture of the character to whom they can relate. This can lead to a great book discussion!

Connection Cards

Copy Connection Cards (page 37) onto cardstock and laminate for durability. Cut out the cards. Then copy Connection Cards Recording Sheet (page 38). Have each student select a card (or give him or her one) and complete a connection sentence using the recording sheet. Alternatively, each student can use a response journal to write his or her entry. Students can also use these cards to make personal responses to independent reading books.

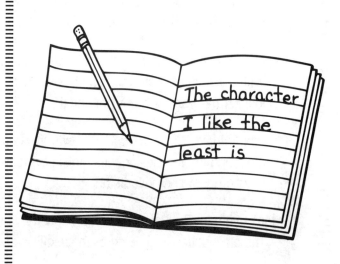

Name _____ Date _____

This Reminds Me . . .

Directions: Begin reading a book. Write down your thoughts about the story, and make two connections below.

Types of Connections

text-to-text = relates to something you read   **text-to-self** = relates to yourself

text-to-world = relates to something that happened in the world

---

Book Title: _____

I read about . . .

_____

_____

_____

_____

_____

This is a **text-to-**_____
connection.

This reminds me . . .

_____

_____

_____

_____

_____

text   self   world
(Circle one.)

I read about . . .

_____

_____

_____

_____

_____

This is a **text-to-**_____
connection.

This reminds me . . .

_____

_____

_____

_____

_____

text   self   world
(Circle one.)

Connecting to Characters

Directions: Read a book. Draw a picture of a character from your story that you can relate to in some way. Then answer the questions about your character.

Book Title: _____

_____

What is your character's name?

_____

How is this character like you?

_____

_____

_____

What personality traits do you have in common? _____

_____

_____

What do you like about this character? _____

_____

_____

If you were this character in the story, how would you feel? Why?

_____

_____

_____

_____

Connection Cards

This part reminds me of . . .	This part makes me feel . . .	I can picture . . .
Something interesting that happens is . . .	This part makes me wonder . . .	A problem that the characters face is . . .
I can relate to this character because . . .	The thing I don't understand is . . .	What I think will happen is . . .
My favorite part so far is . . .	The character I like the least is . . .	This part makes me think of . . .
One of the funniest parts is . . .	I was nervous when . . .	The description of this part was . . .

Name _____ Date _____

Connection Cards
Recording Sheet

Directions: Use your connection card to write about what you read.

Book Title: _____

_____

_____

_____

_____

_____

- -

Name _____ Date _____

Connection Cards
Recording Sheet

Directions: Use your connection card to write about what you read.

Book Title: _____

_____

_____

_____

_____

Summarizing

Being able to concisely summarize what one has read is a critical strategy every reader needs to master. In this section, teachers will be able to strengthen their students' abilities to summarize text. Each of the following activities will help students discover and write about the main ideas of a story.

Suggested Books for Teaching Summarizing

Bunting, Eve. *The Wednesday Surprise.* New York: Clarion Books, 1989.
An overjoyed granddaughter teaches her grandmother to read.

Cannon, Janell. *Verdi.* San Diego, CA: Harcourt, 1997.
Verdi, a proud, fun-loving python, resists the fact that he's aging.

Creech, Sharon. *A Fine, Fine School.* New York: HarperCollins, 2001.
Tillie's principal is a little too enthusiastic about school. He wants to do away with weekends and summer vacation! Only Tillie can tell him he's gone too far.

Henkes, Kevin. *Chrysanthemum.* New York: Greenwillow Books, 1991.
From the first day of school, Chrysanthemum is teased about her unique name. Thankfully, she is well-loved and supported by her family.

Lester, Helen. *Three Cheers for Tacky.* Boston: Houghton Mifflin, 1994.
Tacky enters the Penguin Cheering Contest and ends up leading his squad to victory.

Activities for Summarizing

"HIP" Summaries

With "HIP" Summaries (pages 41–42), your students will be the hippest summarizers in town. After reading a story, pass out a copy of "HIP" Summaries to each student. On page 41, students will write the *who, what, where, when,* and *why* of the story on the hippos. Then on page 42, they will write a paragraph using the information written on the hippos. Use these pages over and over again to provide ample summarizing practice.

What?

Summary Signs

Your students will be able to show you signs that they understand how to summarize with Summary Signs (page 43). This activity can be used with any book. First, make a copy of the page for each student. Have students read a book and then fill in the summary signs using complete sentences and correct punctuation. With this activity, students will become confident with their summary-writing abilities. Use it repeatedly to allow students practice with this skill.

"What Happened?" Chapter Summaries

This activity allows students to continue to practice writing excellent summaries. Provide students with a text that is full of high-interest material. Then provide each student with a copy of "What Happened?" Chapter Summaries (page 44). Have students write their summaries on the page. Your students are sure to be successful summarizers with this added practice.

"HIP" Summaries

Directions: Read a book, and then write the *who, what, where, when,* and *why* of the story on the hippos below.

Book Title: _____

When?

Why?

Where?

Who?

What?

"HIP" Summaries *(cont.)*

Directions: Look at each part of your "HIP" summary on page 41. Now write each part as a complete sentence in a paragraph below. Don't forget to include all of the "HIP" parts!

Book Title: _____

_____

_____

_____

_____

_____

_____

_____

_____

_____

                               _____

                               _____

                               _____

                               _____

                               _____

                               _____

                               _____

Summary Signs

Directions: Read a book, and then write the *who*, *what*, *where*, *when*, and *why* of the story in the signs below.

Book Title: _____

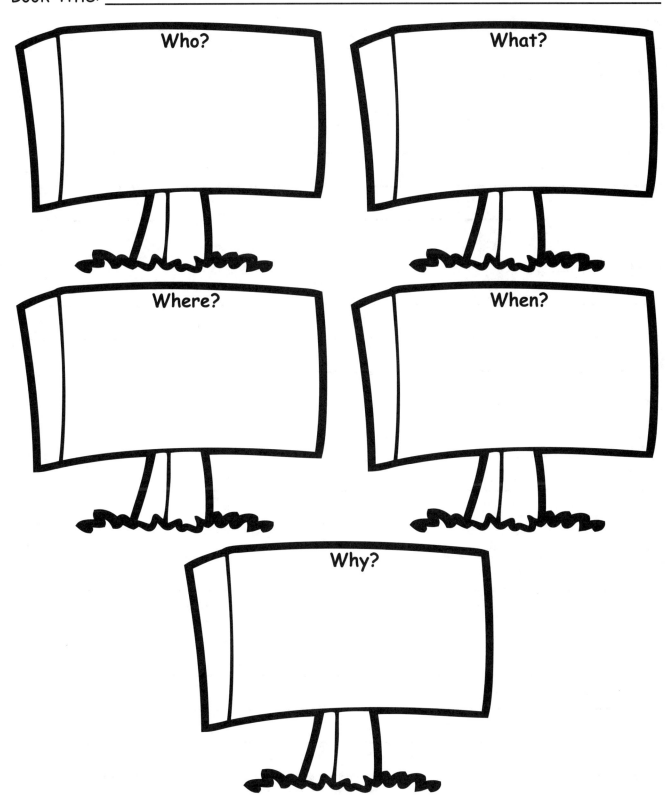

Name _____   Date _____

"What Happened?" Chapter Summaries

Directions: Read a book, and then write one or two sentences summarizing what happened in each chapter you read.

Book Title: _____

Chapter _____

_____

_____

_____

_____

Chapter _____

_____

_____

_____

_____

Chapter _____

_____

_____

_____

_____

Chapter _____

_____

_____

_____

_____

Sequencing

Understanding the order of a story is a skill that is essential for strong readers. In this section, students will be able to practice putting the events of a story in sequence from the beginning to the end. Fun activities and reproducibles will help students master story timelines.

Suggested Books for Teaching Sequencing

Bloom, Becky. *Wolf!* New York: Orchard Books, 1999.
> A hungry wolf plans on making a meal of some barnyard animals, but when he goes to attack, the animals ignore him. They're too engrossed in the books they're reading!

Brett, Jan. *The Mitten.* New York: Putnam, 1989.
> Nicki wants his grandmother to knit white mittens for him. She does it, but he loses one in the snow. Several animals make it their new home.

Gaiman, Neil. *The Day I Swapped My Dad for Two Goldfish.* New York: HarperCollins, 2004.
> Nathan's dad is considered to be the ultimate bargaining chip as he's traded back and forth around the neighborhood.

Hakes Noble, Trinka. *The Day Jimmy's Boa Ate the Wash.* New York: Dial Press, 1980.
> During a class field trip, Jimmy's boa constrictor is let loose on a farm. Havoc ensues!

Viorst, Judith. *Alexander and the Terrible, Horrible, No Good, Very Bad Day.* New York: Atheneum, 1972.
> From the moment he wakes up, Alexander is having a terrible, horrible, no good, very bad day. It is so terrible that he wants to move to Australia!

Activities for Sequencing

Sarah Gets Ready for School

This activity allows students to practice sequencing an unknown story. To begin, make a copy of Sarah Gets Ready for School (pages 47–48) for each student. Have each student cut out the cards and sequence them in the correct order. Then have students glue each card in the appropriate box on the sequencing page. Students will have a great time helping Sarah get ready for school!

Sequence-a-Story Booklet

Your students will be able to practice sequencing by putting together booklets that retell a story in order. To begin this project, copy Sequence-a-Story Booklet (pages 49–51) for each student. Copy as many sequence boxes as needed for your students to retell the story. For example, if six sequence boxes are not enough for your students, try eight, replacing "In the end" on the third page with "Later." Have your students retell the story, in order, on the lines in each box, adding art as they go. Then have them cut out the boxes and staple them together in order to create their story booklets.

Squiggly Sequencing

This is another creative sequencing activity that allows students to practice their sequencing skills. This activity can be used with any book. To begin, copy Squiggly Sequencing (page 52) for each student. After reading a text, students will write the beginning, middle, and end of the story in complete sentences in the boxes provided.

Sarah Gets Ready for School

Directions: Read the cards below. Cut them out, and then glue them in the correct order on page 48.

She put on a pretty red sweater and a blue denim skirt.

Sarah woke up early this morning.

Next, she put on her white socks and red, sparkly shoes. Now she was all dressed!

Sarah got out of bed and walked downstairs for breakfast.

Finally, she grabbed her backpack and headed to the bus stop.

After dressing herself, she went into the bathroom to brush her hair.

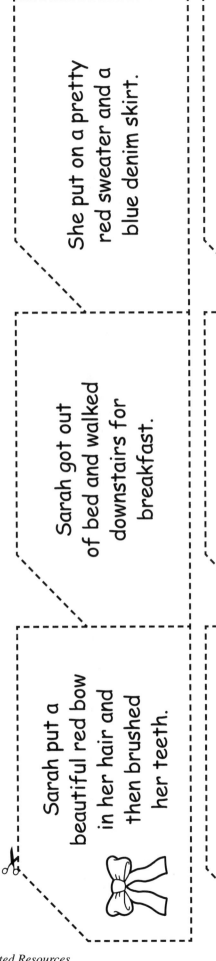

Sarah put a beautiful red bow in her hair and then brushed her teeth.

After breakfast, Sarah went back upstairs to get dressed.

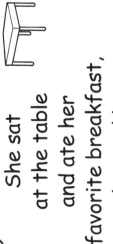

She sat at the table and ate her favorite breakfast, pancakes and bacon.

Sarah Gets Ready for School *(cont.)*

Directions: Read the cards on page 47. Cut them out, and then glue them in the correct order below.

1	2	3

4	5	6

7	8	9

Sequence-a-Story Booklet

Directions: Read a book, and then retell the story, in order, on the lines in each box. Add art to each story box. Then cut out the boxes and staple them together to create your story booklet.

My Story Retelling of

_____

Story by: _____

Retelling by: _____

In the beginning,

_____

_____

_____

_____

Sequence-a-Story Booklet *(cont.)*

Directions: Continue retelling the story (from page 49), in order, on the lines in each box. Then cut out the boxes and staple them together to create your story booklet.

Then,

_____

_____

_____

_____

Next,

_____

_____

_____

_____

Sequence-a-Story Booklet *(cont.)*

Directions: Continue retelling the story (from pages 49 and 50), in order, on the lines in each box. Then cut out the boxes and staple them together to create your story booklet.

Afterwards,

_____

_____

_____

_____

In the end,

_____

_____

_____

_____

Squiggly Sequencing

Directions: Read a book, and then summarize the beginning, middle, and end of the story in complete sentences in the boxes below.

Book Title: _____

Middle

End

Beginning

Retelling

As a component of sequencing, retelling a story with detail can be a difficult task. Nonetheless, retelling is a skill required of any keen reader. With these activities and resources, teachers can help students identify the needed elements of a good retelling. With practice, students will learn to recall story details and write retellings using time-order words.

Suggested Books for Teaching Retelling

Clement, Rod. *Grandpa's Teeth.* New York: HarperCollins, 1997.
Grandpa's false teeth have been stolen, and he suspects everyone has taken them.

Long, Melinda. *How I Became a Pirate.* San Diego, CA: Harcourt, 2003.
Jeremy thinks that being a pirate is fun; however, he eventually misses the comforts of home.

Munsch, Robert. *Paper Bag Princess.* Toronto: Annick Press, 1980.
Elizabeth is a beautiful princess who is about to live "happily ever after" with Prince Ronald until a dragon gets in the way.

Rathmann, Peggy. *Ruby the Copycat.* New York: Scholastic, 1991.
Ruby wants nothing more than to fit in, so she copies the way her friend dresses. Ruby's teacher shows her how to be herself.

Young, Ed. *Lon Po Po.* New York: Philomel Books, 1989.
Lon Po Po, the Granny Wolf, pretends to be the grandmother of three young girls. When one girl realizes "she" is a wolf, they lead the wolf up a tree and over a limb to its death.

Activities for Retelling

Sweet Retellings

Nothing will be sweeter than when your students are having fun using this creative activity. Provide a copy of Sweet Retellings (pages 55–56) for each student. Have students cut out the candy pattern and each circle. After they cut out each piece, students will complete a retelling using any book. When their retellings have been written in the correct spaces, students will glue (or staple) their circles at the top in order to create one complete candy piece. For added fun, students can decorate their candy pieces by wrapping colored plastic wrap around them.

Fly Away with Retellings

Your students will soar above the rest while retelling stories with this activity. To begin, copy Fly Away with Retellings (pages 57–58) for each student. After reading any story, students will write their retellings on the bows of the kites. Then they will cut out the kite patterns and the bows. The final steps are for each student to attach a piece of yarn to the back of the kite pattern and then attach each bow to the remainder of the string. For added fun, have each student color and decorate the kite. Display each kite on a bulletin board titled "Fly Away with Retellings."

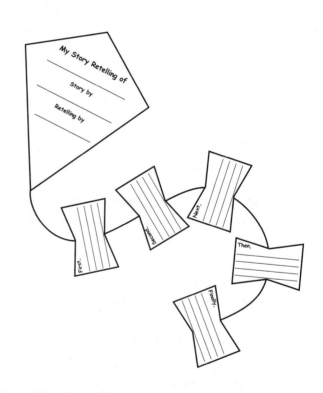

Retelling, from Seed to Sprout

This activity can be used with any story. First, make a copy of Retelling, from Seed to Sprout (page 59) for every student. After reading a story, students will write what happened in the beginning, what happened next, and what happened in the end. This should be written in complete sentences. Your students are sure to become excellent retellers with this practice page.

Sweet Retellings

Directions: Read a book, and then retell the story on the lines below. Cut out the candy pattern and each circle from page 56. Glue the circles at the top to create one complete candy piece.

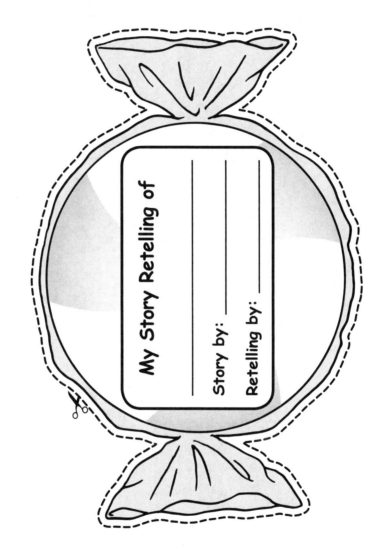

My Story Retelling of

_____
_____
_____

Story by: _____

Retelling by: _____

Sweet Retellings (cont.)

Directions: Cut out the candy pattern on page 55 and each circle below. After cutting out each piece, complete a retelling using any book. When the retellings have been written in the correct spaces, glue the circles at the top to create one complete candy piece.

Finally,

Next,

Then,

In the beginning,

Fly Away with Retellings

Directions: Read a book, and then write a retelling on the bows of the kite. Cut out the kite pattern below and the bows on page 58. Attach a piece of yarn to the back of the kite pieces. Now you have a retelling kite!

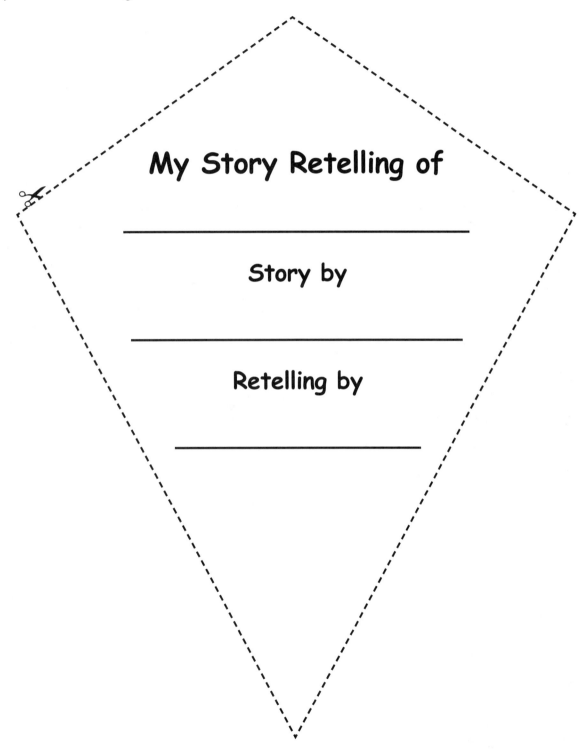

My Story Retelling of

_____

Story by

_____

Retelling by

_____

Fly Away with Retellings *(cont.)*

Directions: Read a book, and then write a retelling on the bows of the kite. Cut out the kite pattern on page 57 and the bows below. Attach a piece of yarn to the back of the kite pieces. Now you have a retelling kite!

First,

Second,

Next,

Then,

Finally,

Retelling, from Seed to Sprout

Directions: Read a book, and then write what happened in the beginning, what happened next, and finally what happened in the end. Use complete sentences, and let your thoughts grow!

Book Title: _____

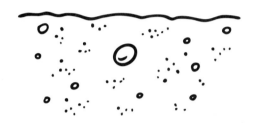

In the beginning,

_____

_____

_____

_____

Then,

_____

_____

_____

_____

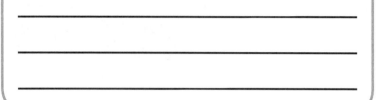

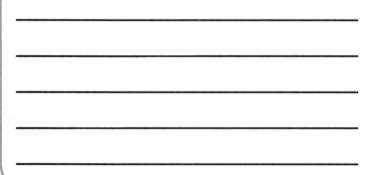

In the end,

_____

_____

_____

_____

Discovering the Main Idea

Discovering the main idea is a skill that is fundamental to basic reading comprehension. Using the activities and reproducibles in this section will help students find the main ideas and supporting details within any type of text.

Suggested Books for Teaching Main Idea

Houston, Gloria. *My Great-Aunt Arizona.* New York: HarperCollins, 1992.
  As a child, Arizona loved to dream of faraway places. Although Arizona goes away to school, she returns to teach in the exact same schoolhouse where she herself learned.

Polacco, Patricia. *The Keeping Quilt.* New York: Simon & Schuster, 1988.
  To celebrate her family's Russian heritage, Anna's mother makes a quilt using old clothing. The quilt is used during many important events.

Shannon, David. *A Bad Case of Stripes.* New York: Blue Sky Press, 1998.
  Camilla really wants to fit in, but two problems prevent her from doing so: 1) Her skin can suddenly turn red, white, and blue; and 2) She likes lima beans.

Silverstein, Shel. *The Giving Tree.* New York: HarperCollins, 1964.
  The tree and the boy are happy companions until the boy demands too much of the tree. In the end, they become happy companions once more.

Williams, Vera. *A Chair for My Mother.* New York: Greenwillow Books, 1982.
  After a family loses their furniture in a fire, they save all of their change in a jar to buy a new chair.

Activities for Discovering the Main Idea

Main Idea Keyrings

This unique graphic organizer can be used with any book, fiction or nonfiction! Copy Main Idea Keyrings (page 62), one per student. To help students find the main idea and supporting details, select a book to read together. After reading the text and pointing out specific ideas, have students use the text to find the main idea of the book, or paragraph, and write down three supporting details. This is great main-idea practice!

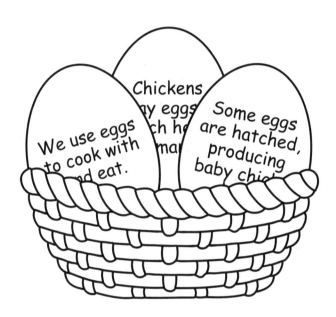

"Egg"cellent Main Ideas

This activity will crack up your students as they read fun facts about eggs. Copy "Egg"cellent Main Ideas (pages 63–64) for each student. Have students read each of the three facts (from page 63) and cut out and glue the correct main-idea basket (from page 64) below the eggs. Your students will be "eggs"tremely aware of main ideas after doing this activity!

Main Ideas from Outer Space

This main-idea activity will have your students finding the difference between main ideas and supporting details. Copy Main Ideas from Outer Space (pages 65–66) for each student. Have students cut out each of the main ideas and supporting details. Students will match the main idea and its supporting details and then glue their results onto Main Ideas from Outer Space (page 66). This activity will help students identify the difference between these types of sentences.

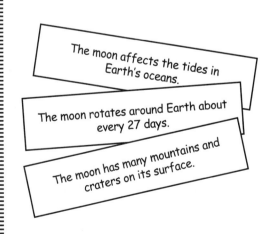

Name _____ Date _____

Main Idea Keyrings

Directions: Read a book, and then write the story's main idea and supporting details in the circles below.

Book Title: _____

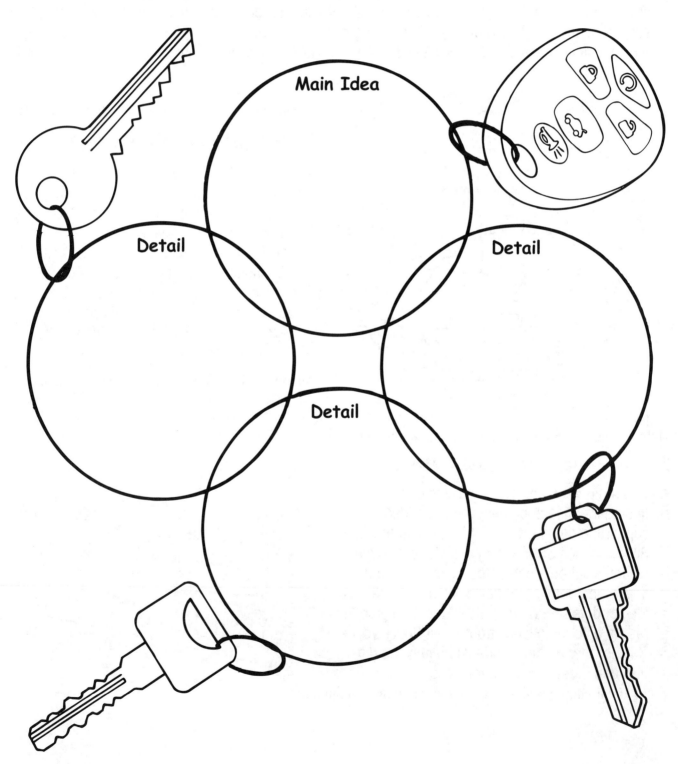

Main Idea

Detail

Detail

Detail

Name _____   Date _____

"Egg"cellent Main Ideas

Directions: Cut out and glue each of the correct main-idea baskets from page 64 below. Be sure the main-idea baskets match with the three facts.

Chickens lay eggs, which helps humans.

We use eggs to cook with and eat.

Some eggs are hatched, producing baby chicks.

Eggs can be poached and served with toast.

Eggs can be beaten to make scrambled eggs.

Eggs can be fried and served with fruit.

The hen lays her fertilized eggs.

The hen sits on the egg while the baby chick grows inside.

After 21 days, the chick hatches from the egg.

Eggs are put into cake and cookie recipes.

Eggs are used in some sauces and dressings.

Eggs are used to make French toast and cheesecake.

The first chickens may have come here on Columbus' ship.

Columbus, an Italian, brought chickens to feed his crew.

The Italian Leghorn chicken lays the eggs we eat.

In China, red-colored eggs are given to new parents.

In Mexico, eggshells are broken and used for confetti.

In Germany, green-colored eggs symbolize a loss of life.

"Egg"cellent Main Ideas *(cont.)*

Directions: Cut out and glue each of the correct main-idea baskets below the eggs on page 63. Be sure the main-idea baskets match with the three facts.

Eggs are used in different ways around the world.

The life cycle of an egg is a fascinating process.

Eggs serve many purposes.

Eggs are a part of many recipes.

Eggs can be cooked in various ways.

Did you ever wonder where chickens came from?

Main Ideas from Outer Space

Directions: Cut out the sentences below and read them carefully. Decide if they are main ideas or supporting details. Then glue the sentences in the correct boxes on page 66.

Jupiter has a giant spot, called the "Giant Red Spot," that is actually a storm.	The moon rotates around Earth about every 27 days.
Each planet in the solar system has very unique features.	The moon has many mountains and craters on its surface.
Earth only has one moon, unlike other planets in the solar system.	Mars has the largest volcanic mountain in the entire solar system.
The moon affects the tides in Earth's oceans.	Saturn is surrounded by many rings, which are made up mostly of water and ice.

Main Ideas from Outer Space

Directions: Cut out the sentences below and read them carefully. Decide if they are main ideas or supporting details. Then glue the sentences in the correct boxes on page 66.

Jupiter has a giant spot, called the "Giant Red Spot," that is actually a storm.	The moon rotates around Earth about every 27 days.
Each planet in the solar system has very unique features.	The moon has many mountains and craters on its surface.
Earth only has one moon, unlike other planets in the solar system.	Mars has the largest volcanic mountain in the entire solar system.
The moon affects the tides in Earth's oceans.	Saturn is surrounded by many rings, which are made up mostly of water and ice.

Main Ideas from Outer Space *(cont.)*

Directions: Cut out the sentences on page 65 and read them carefully. Decide if they are main ideas or supporting details. Then glue the sentences in the correct boxes below.

Main Idea #1

Main Idea #2

Supporting Details

Supporting Details

Understanding Characterization

This section can help students grasp a necessary reading skill: identifying the character traits of main and supporting characters in the stories they read. These activities will give students different ways of looking at book characters. Whether describing their appearances or analyzing their personalities, students will soon understand characters from the inside out!

Suggested Books for Teaching Characterization

Cooney, Barbara. *Miss Rumphius.* New York: Viking Press, 1982.
   With the goal of making the world more beautiful, Miss Rumphius scatters lupine seeds, transforming the rocky landscape around her home.

Henkes, Kevin. *A Weekend with Wendell.* New York: Greenwillow Books, 1986.
   Sophie and her parents cannot wait until Wendell, the troublemaker, goes home—that is, until Sophie realizes that Wendell isn't so bad after all.

Hoffman, Mary. *Amazing Grace.* New York: Dial Books, 1991.
   Grace, a young girl who has an active imagination, wants to play the lead in *Peter Pan.* Her classmates tease her, but her family remains supportive.

Palatini, Margie. *Broom Mates.* New York: Hyperion, 2003.
   Gritch the Witch is preparing for her Halloween party. Will her sister, Mag the Hag, be a help or a hindrance?

Polacco, Patricia. *Thank You, Mr. Falker.* New York: Philomel Books, 1998.
   Trisha is eager to learn, but she finds that words "wiggle" on the page. Her classmates tease her for this. Luckily, Mr. Falker, her teacher, is there to help.

Activities for Understanding Characterization

Character Faces

This activity gives students the opportunity to look into a character's head. After reading a story that has wonderful characterization in it, copy and pass out Character Faces (page 69) to each student. Have students cut out the oval shape, or head, and answer the questions about a character from a story. Then have students flip over the circle, to the blank side, and draw the face of that same character. For fun, copy this activity on paper of different skin colors.

Visualizing a Character

Character development is essential to reading and writing. This activity will allow students to dig deep into well-developed characters. After students have read a story with at least one strong character, give them a copy of Visualizing a Character (page 70). On this page, have students draw the character in the large oval. Then, in the boxes, have students write about the character's personality traits, as well as how the character feels, acts, and thinks.

Character Thoughts

This page can be used two different ways. It can be used during or after reading a story that has well-developed characters. To begin, copy Character Thoughts (page 71) for each student. If students are using this page while reading a book, then have them draw their characters and write what their characters are thinking at that time. If students are using this page after reading the book, then have them draw their characters and write what their characters were thinking at any point during the book (e.g., before or after a problem). Copy this page again and again so that students can repeatedly write down their characters' thoughts.

Name _____   Date _____

Character Faces

Directions: Read a book, and then cut out the oval shape below. Answer the questions about a character from the story. Then flip over the oval, to the blank side, and draw the face of that same character. Now you've really looked into the character's head!

Describe
Your Character

Book Title: _____

Character's Name: _____

What does this character **look like**?

_____

_____

_____

_____

How does this character **behave**?

_____

_____

_____

_____

What does the character **feel** throughout the book?

_____

_____

_____

_____

Visualizing a Character

Directions: Read a book, and then choose one strong character from the story. Draw the character in the large oval. Then in the boxes, write about the character's personality traits, as well as how the character feels, acts, and thinks.

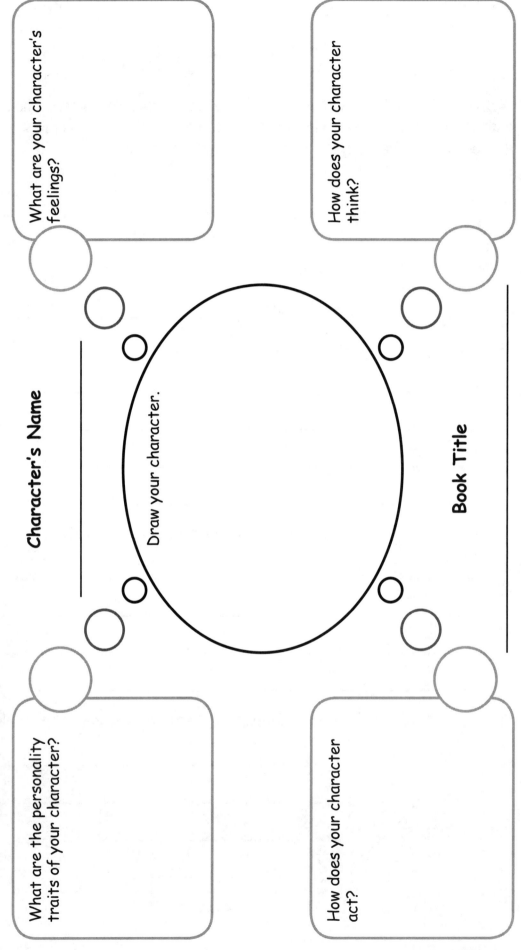

What are your character's feelings?

How does your character think?

Character's Name

Draw your character.

Book Title

What are the personality traits of your character?

How does your character act?

Character Thoughts

Directions: Read a book, and then draw a character from the story in the box. Write what your character is thinking in the thought bubble.

Book Title: _____

Character's Name: _____

Describing the Setting

Beyond naming the place where a story happens, many students have trouble describing the setting, yet doing so is an invaluable skill for reading comprehension. The activities in this section will have students feeling as though they are interacting with the setting. Students will be able to use their senses to tell others about the wondrous places books can take them.

Suggested Books for Teaching Setting

Fleischman, Paul. *Weslandia.* Cambridge, MA: Candlewick Press, 1999.
    Wesley is spending his summer doing something other children won't be doing—he is caring for a unique and wondrous plant.

Polacco, Patricia. *Thunder Cake.* New York: Philomel Books, 1990.
    As a storm approaches, a grandmother helps her granddaughter overcome her fear of thunder by baking a special kind of cake.

Sendak, Maurice. *Where the Wild Things Are.* New York: HarperCollins, 1963.
    Max, a mischievous boy, is sent to bed without supper. In his room, his mind wanders to a world where the wild things are.

Van Allsburg, Chris. *Jumanji.* Boston: Houghton Mifflin, 1981.
    Judy and Peter play a jungle-adventure board game that has them hiding from lions and sleeping from tsetse-fly bites.

Yolen, Jane. *Owl Moon.* New York: Philomel Books, 1987.
    On a moonlit winter night, a girl and her father take a walk and look for owls.

Activities for Describing the Setting

Setting the Mood

Copy Setting the Mood (page 74) for each student. After reading a story that has a well-developed setting, students can practice visualizing-, mood-, and setting-identification skills with this activity. First, have students draw a detailed picture of the main character in the setting of the book. Then have them answer the questions that relate to the mood of the story. Your students will be able to interpret moods from their drawings and understand how they relate to the settings.

Taking the Lid Off the Setting

This activity allows students to look closely at a setting from a story. Copy Taking the Lid Off the Setting (page 75) for each student. After students read a story, have them close their eyes and think about all the things they can see in the setting. Also, have them visualize all the things they can feel, hear, and smell. Have students practice putting themselves in the setting and making inferences based on the story and their prior knowledge. Teachers can use The Details Are in the Setting (page 76) the same way to provide more practice for students.

The Details Are in the Setting

This is another activity that will allow students to delve into the setting of a story. To do this activity, students have to use their "imaginary" senses as if they are standing in the middle of the setting. To begin, copy The Details Are in the Setting (page 76) for each student. After students read a story, have them fill in the *see*, *hear*, *feel*, and *smell* boxes. Each student will also need to draw a picture of a character in the setting. Teachers can use Taking the Lid Off the Setting (page 75) the same way to provide more practice for students.

Name _____ Date _____

Setting the Mood

Directions: Read a book, and then draw a detailed picture of the main character in the setting. Answer the questions that relate to the mood of the story at the bottom of the page.

Book Title: _____

Where does the story take place? _____

_____

How does the character feel in this setting? _____

_____

Describe the mood of the story: _____

What are some things in the setting that show this mood? _____

_____

How would you feel in this type of setting? _____

Name _____   Date _____

Taking the Lid Off the Setting

Directions: Read a book, and then close your eyes and think about the setting. What can you see, feel, hear, and smell? Write down your responses in the boxes below.

Book Title: _____

What can you see?	What can you feel?
What can you hear?	**What can you smell?**

The Details Are in the Setting

Directions: Read a book, and then close your eyes and think about the setting. What can you see, feel, hear, and smell? Write down your responses in the boxes below. Then draw a picture of a character in the setting.

Book Title: _____

See?	Draw your character in the setting.
Feel?	
Hear?	
Smell?	Character's Name _____

Finding the Problem and the Solution

This section focuses on a fundamental skill—finding the problem and the solution. The provided matching and sorting activities allow children to practice focusing on the problem and solution of an unknown literature selection. The graphic organizer can also be reproduced and used many times with different texts. Students will be able to identify many problems and solutions using these various activities.

Suggested Books for Teaching Problem and Solution

Bang, Molly. *When Sophie Gets Angry—Really, Really Angry.* New York: Blue Sky Press, 1999.
Sophie is angry because her sister wants to play with a favorite stuffed gorilla. When Mom sides with her sister, Sophie runs away until she calms down.

Brett, Jan. *Trouble with Trolls.* New York: G. P. Putnam's Sons, 1992.
When some trolls try to kidnap Treva's dog, Treva outwits them.

Munsch, Robert. *Andrew's Loose Tooth.* New York: Scholastic, 1998.
Everyone is trying to yank out Andrew's loose tooth, but only one thing makes it come out of his mouth: a sneeze!

Palatini, Margie. *Piggie Pie!* New York: Clarion Books, 1995.
Gritch the Witch needs pigs for her pie, but when she arrives at the farm, all she finds is a wolf.

Yolen, Jane. *Piggins.* New York: Harcourt, 1987.
Piggins, a butler, ends up being the hero of an elite dinner party when he solves a crime that took place that evening.

Activities for Finding the Problem and the Solution

Monkeying Around with a Problem

This activity will make students go bananas for story problems! Copy Monkeying Around with a Problem (page 79) for each student. Have students begin reading a story that has a clear problem. Have them stop reading once they get to the main problem in the story. Next, have students fill out the top portion of the graphic organizer. Then have students do the next part on their own. Students will draw a picture showing how they think the problem will be solved. Have them continue reading the story to the end. Once they complete the story, have them evaluate their predictions in the final box.

Problem and Solution Cookie Jars

Copy Problem and Solution Cookie Jars (page 80) onto tan-colored paper for each student. Then copy Problem and Solution Cookie Jars Recording Sheet (page 81), one per student. Give each student a piece of 8½" x 11" paper and have them fold it in half, length-wise. Have students outline the shape of a cookie jar on each side of the page. Then have them cut out and glue the problem and solution labels on each side of the folded paper so that each cookie jar is labeled as either a "Problem" or "Solution" cookie jar. Have students read the cookies and match the problems to their solutions. Then have them glue the "cookies" into the cookie jars and record the matches on the recording sheets.

The next day, Tim and Jake arrive at school ready to take the test. In the middle of the science test, Jake's pencil breaks, but he cannot get out of his chair.

He raises his hand quietly and waits for his teacher to arrive.

Problems and Solutions in the Sky

Your students will soar away with problems and solutions using this fun activity! Copy Problems and Solutions in the Sky (page 82) for each student. Have students cut out each star and cloud and read each problem and solution. Then have students match the problems to their solutions and put them in order (in pairs and as a whole). At this point, once the clouds are in order, students can either glue the shapes onto a piece of blue construction paper or hole-punch the top of the shapes and tie them together using yarn. If choosing the latter, you may wish to hang the mobiles from a bulletin board or the ceiling for a fun visual decoration.

Name _____ Date _____

Monkeying Around with a Problem

Directions: Begin reading a book, and then stop reading once you get to the main problem in the story. Fill out the "problem" box and draw a picture of how you think the problem will be solved. Continue reading the story to the end. Then answer the questions in the box at the bottom of the page.

Book Title: _____

Problem

_____

_____

_____

_____

_____

Draw a picture showing how you think the problem will be solved.

How was the problem solved by the characters?

_____

_____

Were your predictions correct? Why or why not?

_____

_____

Problem and Solution Cookie Jars

Directions: Fold a piece of 8½" x 11" paper in half, length-wise. Outline the shape of a cookie jar on each side of the page. Cut out the problem and solution labels at the bottom of the page and glue them on each side of the folded paper so that each cookie jar is labeled as either a "Problem" or "Solution" cookie jar. Cut out and read each "cookie" below, matching the problems to their solutions. Glue the "cookies" into the cookie jars and record your matches on the recording sheet (page 81).

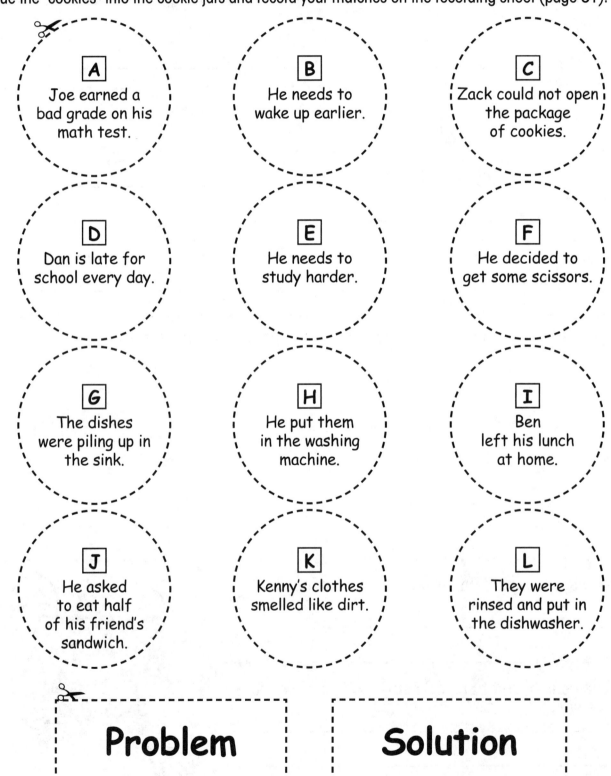

A — Joe earned a bad grade on his math test.

B — He needs to wake up earlier.

C — Zack could not open the package of cookies.

D — Dan is late for school every day.

E — He needs to study harder.

F — He decided to get some scissors.

G — The dishes were piling up in the sink.

H — He put them in the washing machine.

I — Ben left his lunch at home.

J — He asked to eat half of his friend's sandwich.

K — Kenny's clothes smelled like dirt.

L — They were rinsed and put in the dishwasher.

Problem

Solution

Problem and Solution Cookie Jars
Recording Sheet

Directions: Cut out and read each "cookie" from page 80, and then match the problems to their solutions. Glue the "cookies" into the cookie jars, and record your matches on the recording sheet below, using the capital letters on the cookies.

Problem	Solution
_____	_____
_____	_____
_____	_____
_____	_____
_____	_____
_____	_____

- -

Name _____ Date _____

Problem and Solution Cookie Jars
Recording Sheet

Directions: Cut out and read each "cookie" from page 80, and then match the problems to their solutions. Glue the "cookies" into the cookie jars, and record your matches on the recording sheet below, using the capital letters on the cookies.

Problem	Solution
_____	_____
_____	_____
_____	_____
_____	_____
_____	_____

Problems and Solutions in the Sky

Directions: Cut out each star and cloud, and read each problem and solution. Match the problems to their solutions and put them in order (in pairs and as a whole). Then glue the shapes onto a piece of blue construction paper or hole-punch the top of the shapes and tie them together using yarn.

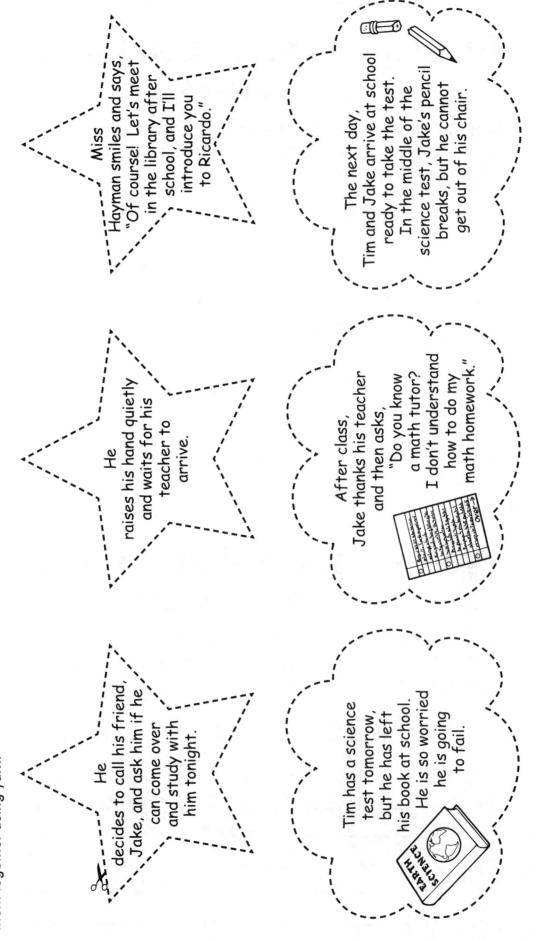

Miss Hayman smiles and says, "Of course! Let's meet in the library after school, and I'll introduce you to Ricardo."

The next day, Tim and Jake arrive at school ready to take the test. In the middle of the science test, Jake's pencil breaks, but he cannot get out of his chair.

He raises his hand quietly and waits for his teacher to arrive.

After class, Jake thanks his teacher and then asks, "Do you know a math tutor? I don't understand how to do my math homework."

He decides to call his friend, Jake, and ask him if he can come over and study with him tonight.

Tim has a science test tomorrow, but he has left his book at school. He is so worried he is going to fail.

Comparing and Contrasting

This reading skill helps students identify similarities and differences within a story or among different texts. Using the reproducible book activities, students will be able to find comparisons throughout the stories they are reading. An additional sorting activity will allow teachers to illustrate this concept using an unknown reading selection.

Suggested Books for Teaching Comparing and Contrasting

Brett, Jan. *Town Mouse, Country Mouse.* New York: G. P. Putnam's Sons, 1994.
   Two city mice swap homes with two country mice in this "grass is always greener" tale.

Cannon, Janell. *Stellaluna.* San Diego, CA: Harcourt, 1993.
   Stellaluna, a bat, is taken in by a bird after being separated from her mother. Mama Bird teaches her uninstinctual behaviors. Stellaluna's mother returns to correct these.

Lowell, Susan. *The Three Javelinas.* Flagstaff, AZ: Northland Publishing, 1992.
   The story of the three little pigs is retold and set in the American Southwest. The pigs are javelinas, or hairy cousins to the pig, and the wolf is a coyote.

Scieszka, Jon. *The True Story of the Three Little Pigs.* New York: Viking Press, 1989.
   Alexander T. Wolf feels that his reputation has been ruined by the three little pigs. He hopes to revive it by telling his side of the story.

Seibert, Patricia. *The Three Little Pigs.* Columbus, OH: School Specialty Publishing, 2002.
   This is the classic tale of the three little pigs.

Trivizas, Eugene. *The Three Little Wolves and the Big Bad Pig.* New York: Margaret K. McElderry Books, 1993.
   Three adorable, young wolves stop an intimidating pig in this twist on the tale of the three little pigs.

Activities for Comparing and Contrasting

"Y" Not Compare?

This graphic organizer can be used with two books to compare character, setting, or even plot. To begin, copy "Y" Not Compare? (page 85), one per student. Have students label each side of the "Y" with the two books they read. Instruct students to write what is different between the books on the top of the "Y." Have them write what is similar on the bottom of the "Y."

Creamy Comparisons

With this graphic organizer, your students will love the taste they get from comparing and contrasting! First, copy Creamy Comparisons (page 86) for each student. Then choose two different books for students to compare and contrast. After reading the selected texts, students will complete the organizer, describing the "differences" between the books in the individual scoops and the "similarities" in the combining scoop. This is a delicious way to practice looking at different parts of texts!

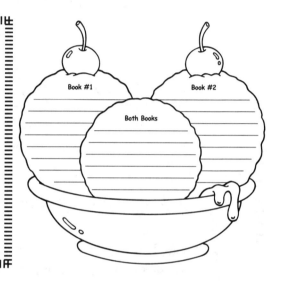

Sea Animal Comparisons

Students can learn as they go with this informational activity. Make a copy of Sea Animal Comparisons (pages 87–88) for every student. Have students read the Sharks and Dolphins passages (page 87) to themselves. Then have them apply their knowledge of what they read to the graphic organizer activity (page 88). Have students cut out the facts about sharks and dolphins on the bottom of the page and glue each fact under the appropriate heading.

"Y" Not Compare?

Directions: Read two books, and then write the titles of the books you are comparing on the lines below. Write what is different between the books on the top of the "Y." Write what is similar on the bottom of the "Y."

Book Title   Book Title

_____   _____

Differences

_____

_____

_____

_____

_____

_____

_____

_____

Differences

_____

_____

_____

_____

_____

_____

_____

_____

Similarities

_____

_____

_____

_____

_____

_____

_____

_____

Creamy Comparisons

Directions: Read two books, and then complete the organizer below. Write the "differences" in the individual scoops and the "similarities" in the combining scoop.

Title of Book #1: _____

Title of Book #2: _____

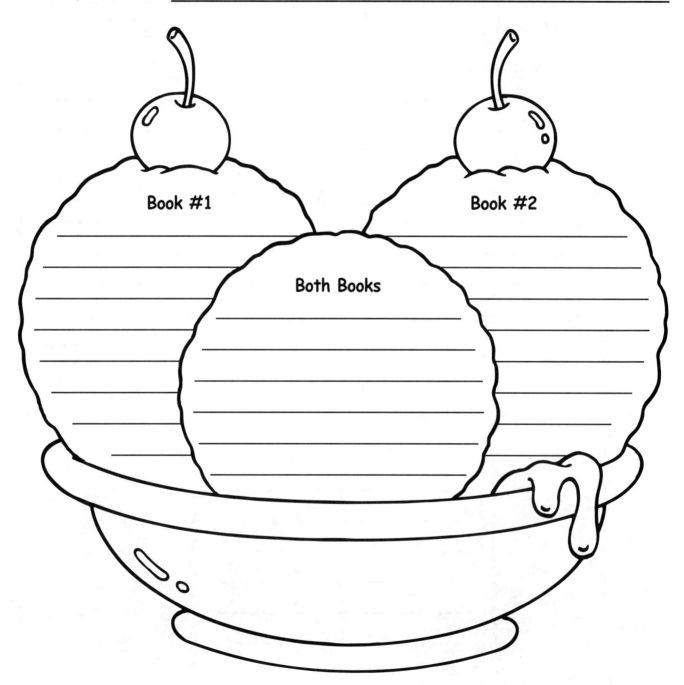

Book #1

Book #2

Both Books

Sea Animal Comparisons

Sharks

Sharks are a type of fish, and most are cold-blooded. They breathe like most fish, through gills on the sides of their heads. Sharks do not have bones. Their bodies are made up of cartilage, which is the flexible material humans have in their ears. Most sharks are meat-eaters, preying on sea animals, such as dolphins, seals, turtles, and other fish. Sharks have many teeth to eat their prey. Sharks also have different fins on their bodies. The top fin is called a dorsal fin, and the tail fin is called the caudal fin. Some sharks lay eggs, while many give birth to live young. Sharks can seem like fierce predators; however, some sharks can be harmless.

Dolphins

Dolphins are warm-blooded mammals that are very intelligent. Being mammals, they breathe air—but dolphins use blowholes on top of their heads. Dolphins like to live in groups and have a distinctive whistle that allows them to communicate with other dolphins. They like to feed on different types of fish and sometimes enjoy eating squid and octopus. Although dolphins have teeth, they do not chew their food. They swallow the fish whole. Dolphins have different fins. The top fin is called a dorsal fin, and the tail fin is called a fluke. Dolphins give birth to live babies. Dolphins can be very friendly creatures!

Sea Animal Comparisons *(cont.)*

Directions: Read the Sharks and Dolphins passages on page 87 to yourself. Then use the passages to help you with the activity below. Cut out the facts about sharks and dolphins at the bottom of the page, and then glue each fact under the correct heading.

Dolphins	Both	Sharks

✂ -

breathe with gills	do not have bones
swallow food whole	live in groups
can give birth to live young	eat different fish
have teeth	Some can lay eggs.
are fish	
are mammals	
have dorsal fins	
are warm-blooded	

Recognizing Cause and Effect

Teachers will be able to help explain cause and effect easily with the various activities in this section. Whether it's through a matching or sorting activity, students will be able to practice identifying specific causes and effects within different stories. An easy-to-use graphic organizer is also included and can be reproduced many times to increase cause-and-effect comprehension.

Suggested Books for Teaching Cause and Effect

Numeroff, Laura. *If You Give a Moose a Muffin.* New York: HarperCollins, 1991.
   What happens when you give a moose a muffin? He will ask for jam, of course! As this story shows, one thing always leads to another.

Peet, Bill. *The Wump World.* Boston: Houghton Mifflin, 1974.
   The Pollutians have overrun the Wump World, forcing the Wumps underground. When the Pollutians leave, the Wumps are left with a concrete jungle.

Saltzman, David. *The Jester Has Lost His Jingle.* Palos Verdes Estates, CA: Jester Company, 1995.
   A court jester wakes up to find that the world is in too much pain to laugh. He works on his routines and eventually restores laughter to the world.

Viorst, Judith. *Alexander, Who Used to Be Rich Last Sunday.* New York: Atheneum, 1978.
   Alexander used to have as much money as Nicholas and Anthony, but then he spent it. Now all he has left are bus tokens.

Wood, Audrey. *The Napping House.* New York: Harcourt, 1984.
   Everyone is piled up on each other and sleeping soundly—until that wakeful flea comes along.

Activities for Recognizing Cause and Effect

Cause and Effect Map

This activity page can be used with any text that contains various examples of cause and effect. First, copy Cause and Effect Map (page 91), one per student. After reading the selected story, students will complete the activity by listing examples of causes and effects and drawing a picture to match each set.

What Caused It?

What Caused It? (page 92) is an interactive practice activity for students to identify cause and effect. Copy the activity page for each student. Have them cut out the different causes and match them to the correct effects. This activity page can be used as an assessment tool to determine your students' abilities to recognize cause and effect.

Cause and Effect Matchup Cards

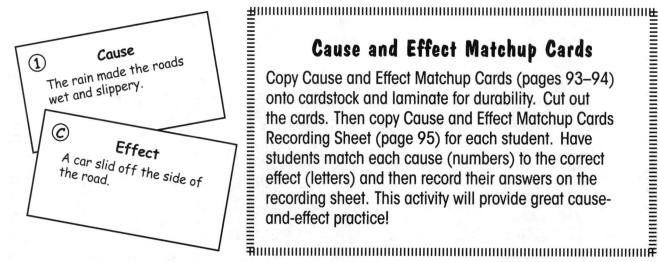

① Cause
The rain made the roads wet and slippery.

Ⓒ Effect
A car slid off the side of the road.

Copy Cause and Effect Matchup Cards (pages 93–94) onto cardstock and laminate for durability. Cut out the cards. Then copy Cause and Effect Matchup Cards Recording Sheet (page 95) for each student. Have students match each cause (numbers) to the correct effect (letters) and then record their answers on the recording sheet. This activity will provide great cause-and-effect practice!

Name _____

Date _____

Cause and Effect Map

Directions: Read a book, and then list examples of causes and effects from the story. Draw a picture in the last box to match each cause-and-effect set.

Book Title: _____

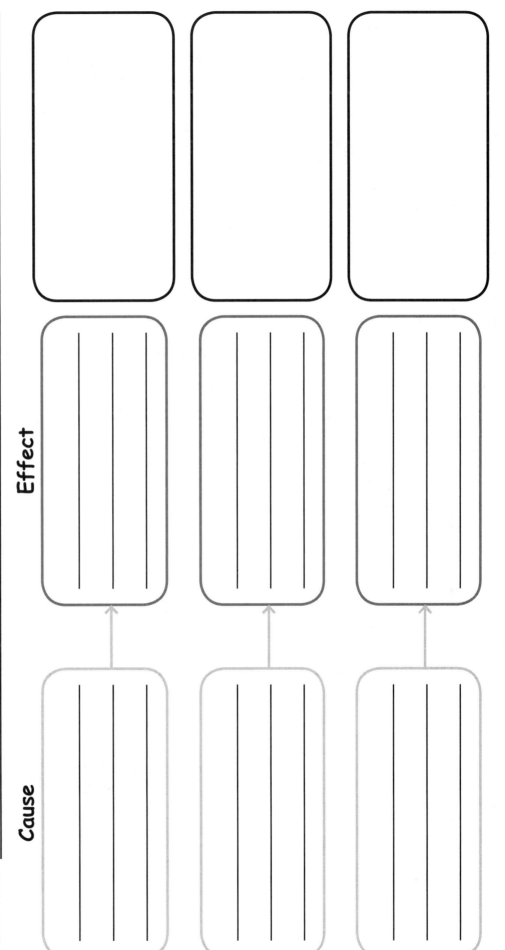

Cause

Effect

What Caused It?

Directions: Read and cut out the different causes below and match them to the correct effects.

Effect	Cause
1. Allison's stomach was growling loudly.	
2. James couldn't complete his homework.	
3. David received an A on his test.	
4. Therese missed out on recess.	
5. Sam had nothing to drink at lunch.	
6. Everyone cheered loudly for Lyla.	
7. Jose cried and ran to the nurse's office.	
8. Cho missed the bus.	

He studied hard.	He fell down and scraped his knee.
He forgot his math book.	She scored a goal in her soccer game.
He spilled his milk on the table.	She forgot to eat breakfast.
She broke a class rule.	She woke up late for school.

Cause and Effect Matchup Cards

① **Cause**

The rain made the roads wet and slippery.

Ⓔ **Effect**

The ball skipped over the hole and went into the lake.

② **Cause**

The golfer sneezed as he hit the ball.

Ⓑ **Effect**

She was grounded for one month and couldn't go to her friend's birthday party.

③ **Cause**

The girl left the water running in the bathtub.

Ⓒ **Effect**

A car slid off the side of the road.

④ **Cause**

The child did not listen to her parents when they asked her to stay home.

Ⓓ **Effect**

A police officer gave him a ticket.

⑤ **Cause**

My dad was late for work, so he sped on the freeway.

Ⓖ **Effect**

Water overflowed onto the floor and soaked the rugs.

Cause and Effect Matchup Cards (cont.)

⑥ **Cause**

The storm was violent. There was thunder and lightning everywhere.

Ⓐ **Effect**

Beautiful flowers began to bloom in the spring.

⑦ **Cause**

The coach made the team practice every day after school.

Ⓕ **Effect**

The boy had a stomachache.

⑧ **Cause**

The boy ate four plates of food and then had some ice cream.

Ⓘ **Effect**

He fell off and hurt his forehead. He had to go to the hospital to get stitches.

⑨ **Cause**

The gardener watered the flower garden every day.

Ⓙ **Effect**

The team began to play well, and they won the big game.

⑩ **Cause**

The boy climbed on top of the couch and started to jump on it.

Ⓗ **Effect**

The dog ran under the bed to hide because it was scared.

Cause and Effect Matchup Cards
Recording Sheet

Directions: Match each cause to the correct effect, and then record your answers below.

Cause Number	Effect Letter
1	
2	
3	
4	
5	
6	
7	
8	
9	
10	

✂ -

Name _____ Date _____

Cause and Effect Matchup Cards
Recording Sheet

Directions: Match each cause to the correct effect, and then record your answers below.

Cause Number	Effect Letter
1	
2	
3	
4	
5	
6	
7	
8	
9	
10	

Answer Key

Page 13

visible: easy to see

frantic: anxious

Page 14

1. find
2. solve
3. shirt
4. searched for

Page 15

1. strong
2. kept
3. dirty
4. find

Pages 16–17

1. sad
2. looked
3. chased
4. careful
5. hungry
6. great pain
7. very excited
8. bother
9. save
10. hide

Pages 18–19

scampered: moved quickly

enormous: huge

gnaw: chew

vibration: noise

discomfort: pain

descended: went down

hurdled: jumped

Pages 23–25

1. A cave
2. A carnival
3. The ocean
4. The park
5. The desert
6. A birthday party
7. A car
8. A restaurant

Pages 47–48

1. Sarah woke up early this morning.
2. Sarah got out of bed and walked downstairs for breakfast.
3. She sat at the table and ate her favorite breakfast, pancakes and bacon.
4. After breakfast, Sarah went back upstairs to get dressed.
5. She put on a pretty red sweater and a blue denim skirt.

6. Next, she put on her white socks and red, sparkly shoes. Now she was all dressed!
7. After dressing herself, she went into the bathroom to brush her hair.
8. Sarah put a beautiful red bow in her hair and then brushed her teeth.
9. Finally, she grabbed her backpack and headed to the bus stop.

Pages 63–64

1. Eggs serve many purposes.
2. Eggs can be cooked in various ways.
3. The life cycle of an egg is a fascinating process.
4. Eggs are a part of many recipes.
5. Did you ever wonder where chickens came from?
6. Eggs are used in different ways around the world.

Pages 65–66

Main Idea #1

Each planet in the solar system has very unique features.

Supporting Details

- Jupiter has a giant spot, called the "Giant Red Spot," that is actually a storm.
- Saturn is surrounded by many rings, which are made up mostly of water and ice.
- Mars has the largest volcanic mountain in the entire solar system.

Main Idea #2

Earth only has one moon, unlike other planets in the solar system.

Supporting Details

- The moon rotates around Earth about every 27 days.
- The moon affects the tides in Earth's oceans.
- The moon has many mountains and craters on its surface.

Pages 80–81

Answer pairs:

A and E

D and B

G and L

C and F

I and J

K and H

Page 82

Problem 1: Tim has a science test tomorrow, but he has left his book at school. He is so worried he is going to fail.

Solution 1: He decides to call his friend, Jake, and ask him if he can come over and study with him tonight.

Problem 2: The next day, Tim and Jake arrive at school ready to take the test. In the middle of the science test, Jake's pencil breaks, but he cannot get out of his chair.

Solution 2: He raises his hand quietly and waits for his teacher to arrive.

Problem 3: After class, Jake thanks his teacher and then asks, "Do you know a math tutor? I don't understand how to do my math homework."

Solution 3: Miss Hayman smiles and says, "Of course! Let's meet in the library after school, and I'll introduce you to Ricardo."

Pages 87–88

Dolphins

- swallow food whole
- live in groups
- are mammals
- are warm-blooded

Both

- have dorsal fins
- have teeth
- can give birth to live young
- eat different fish

Sharks

- do not have bones
- breathe with gills
- are fish
- Some can lay eggs.

Page 92

1. She forgot to eat breakfast.
2. He forgot his math book.
3. He studied hard.
4. She broke a class rule.
5. He spilled his milk on the table.
6. She scored a goal in her soccer game.
7. He fell down and scraped his knee.
8. She woke up late for school.

Pages 93–95

1. C
2. E
3. G
4. B
5. D
6. H
7. J
8. F
9. A
10. I